SPORTS
ALL-STARS

DEREK CARR

Jon M. Fishman

Lerner Publications ◆ Minneapolis

Lerner Publications Company
A division of Lerner Publishing Group, Inc.
241 First Avenue North
Minneapolis, MN 55401 USA

For reading levels and more information, look up this title at www.lernerbooks.com.

Main body text set in Albany Std 15/22. Typeface provided by Agfa.

Library of Congress Cataloging-in-Publication Data

Names: Fishman, Jon M., author.
Title: Derek Carr / Jon M. Fishman.
Description: Minneapolis : Lerner Publications, 2018. | Series: Sports all-stars | Includes bibliographical references and index.
Identifiers: LCCN 2017021595 (print) | LCCN 2017045832 (ebook) | ISBN 9781512482645 (eb pdf) | ISBN 9781512482485 (lb : alk. paper) | ISBN 9781541512016 (pb : alk. paper)
Subjects: LCSH: Carr, Derek, 1991—Juvenile literature. | Quarterbacks (Football)—United States—Biography—Juvenile literature.
Classification: LCC GV939.C3746 (ebook) | LCC GV939.C3746 F57 2018 (print) | DDC 796.332092 [B]—dc23

LC record available at https://lccn.loc.gov/2017021595

Manufactured in the United States of America
1-43297-33117-9/27/2017

CONTENTS

RAIDER LEADER

Derek Carr winds up to pass the ball during a 2016 game against the Buffalo Bills.

Oakland Raiders quarterback Derek Carr stood five yards behind his offensive line. *Hut! Hut!* The **center** snapped the football to Carr. Carr held it high and hopped backward. Then he spotted an open **wide receiver**. Carr launched a pass. Touchdown!

The Raiders were playing catch-up against the Buffalo Bills on December 4, 2016. Carr's touchdown pass made the score Buffalo 24, Oakland 16. The Raiders scored a few minutes later on a running play. They were within one point of Buffalo, 24–23.

Carr looks for a receiver during the game against the Bills.

Carr took over the game in the fourth quarter. He drove the Raiders to Buffalo's 37-yard line. He faked a pass to the right side. Then he let loose a deep pass that arced high above the field. Wide receiver Amari Cooper was there. He snatched the ball out of the air and ran for a touchdown.

The Raiders won the game, 38–24. The victory was their 10th of the season with just two losses. Football is a team sport. Yet Oakland fans knew the team owed much of its success to their star quarterback. "It's an exciting time in Oakland," Carr said after the game. "It's definitely fun times."

Carr celebrates a
Raiders touchdown.

Derek's father passed on his love of football to his three sons. Derek's older brother David (*pictured*) was also a football star.

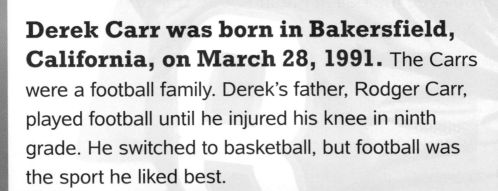

Derek Carr was born in Bakersfield, California, on March 28, 1991. The Carrs were a football family. Derek's father, Rodger Carr, played football until he injured his knee in ninth grade. He switched to basketball, but football was the sport he liked best.

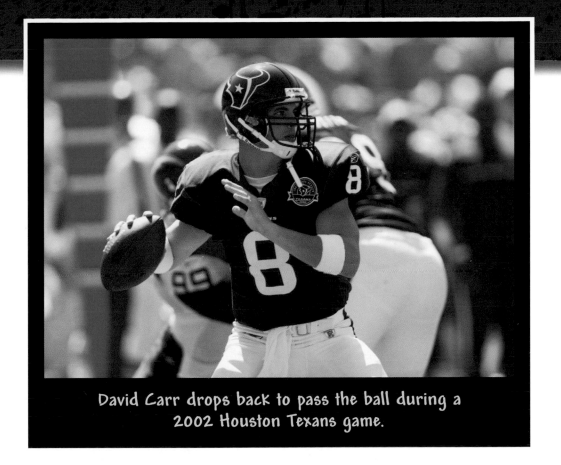

David Carr drops back to pass the ball during a 2002 Houston Texans game.

Carr has two older brothers, David and Darren. David Carr played football at Fresno State University. In 2002, the NFL's Houston Texans chose the quarterback with the first overall pick in the NFL Draft. The Carr family packed up and followed their oldest son to Houston, Texas. Darren Carr played college football and then became the head football coach at Bakersfield Christian High School, in Bakersfield, California.

In Houston, Derek got the chance to see what the life of an NFL player was like. He spent time in the Texans locker room. He saw how the team prepared for games. Derek and his brother watched video of the team's next opponents. Derek even got to play catch with great players, such as wide receiver Andre Johnson. "Then he'd go back and play with his 12-year-old buddies and say, 'This game's easy,'" said David Carr.

During halftime of one Texans game, Derek took the field with his youth team. They faced off in a fun game against a team of **mascots**. Derek played quarterback. On one play, the ball bounced around on the ground.

Derek became the starting quarterback for his high school football team as a sophomore in 2006.

Derek Carr passes the ball during a 2013 college game.

Derek reached for it, but he was too late. He was tackled by a gang of mascots!

After high school, Carr followed in his oldest brother's footsteps and played football at Fresno State. He put up great numbers. Carr threw 26 touchdowns as a sophomore and 37 touchdowns as a junior. In those years combined, he threw just 16 **interceptions**.

Carr married his wife, Heather, in college. On August 5, 2013, their son Dallas Mason Carr was born. But the baby was sick. He kept throwing up. Doctors discovered a problem with his **intestines**. Dallas had three surgeries and spent 23 days in the hospital.

The surgeries worked, and Dallas recovered. His dad played the first game of his senior season for Fresno State the day after Dallas came home from the hospital. He threw five touchdown passes in a win over Rutgers University. For the season, he threw an incredible 50 touchdowns and just 8 interceptions.

Carr had become a top NFL **prospect**. But the NFL career of his oldest brother had not lived up to expectations. Some **scouts** thought that Carr would also have trouble at football's highest level. He wasn't worried. "Everything that we went through in our lives, in my family . . . whatever happens in football, it's just a game," he said.

Carr runs the 40-yard dash at the 2014 NFL Scouting Combine.

In college, Carr proved that he was a world-class athlete. He showed it again at the 2014 NFL Scouting Combine. At the combine, NFL prospects go through a series of tests. Scouts judge the players based on their strength, speed, and much more.

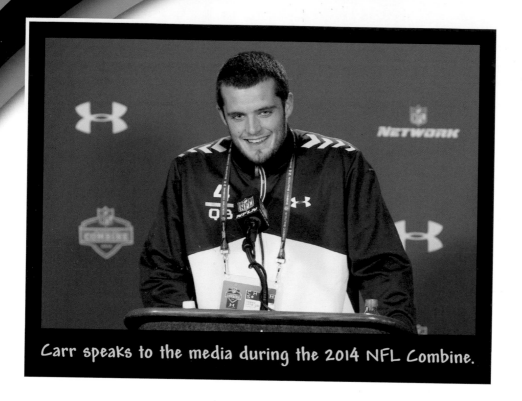

Carr speaks to the media during the 2014 NFL Combine.

Carr dazzled the scouts. He ran the 40-yard dash in 4.69 seconds. That was the fifth-best time among quarterbacks. Then he soared 34.5 inches (88 cm) in the **vertical jump**. The leap was the second best for a quarterback. The Oakland Raiders liked what they saw. They chose Carr with the 36th overall pick in the NFL Draft that year.

Carr had the strength and speed to play in the NFL. Yet he knew from his brother that his work was just beginning. "I had a heads-up [from David] on what I needed to do as a **rookie**," Carr said. "It was literally to go in, work hard, and keep your mouth shut."

Working hard has never been a problem for Carr. He does different exercises to keep his body in shape for football. He quickly lifts light weights many times in a row. This helps his muscles work longer without getting tired. He also lifts heavier weights fewer times to improve how quickly his muscles can move.

Another important part of Carr's fitness routine is football drills. He spends plenty of time throwing balls to fellow players and coaches. He also does exercises such as stepping sideways over pads on the ground. As he steps, he holds a football and keeps his head up. This drill helps Carr find open wide receivers during games.

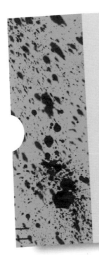

Carr and his oldest brother know that it's important to take part in different exercises. Some of their workouts are pretty unusual. They've even been known to push David Carr's truck through the parking lot to work up a sweat.

In a game against the Indianapolis Colts on December 24, 2016, Carr was tackled from behind. His right foot twisted beneath him. TV cameras caught him saying, "It's broke." He was right. A bone in his lower right leg was broken. Carr's season was over.

Carr had surgery three days later to repair the broken bone. But surgery was just the beginning. Carr faced

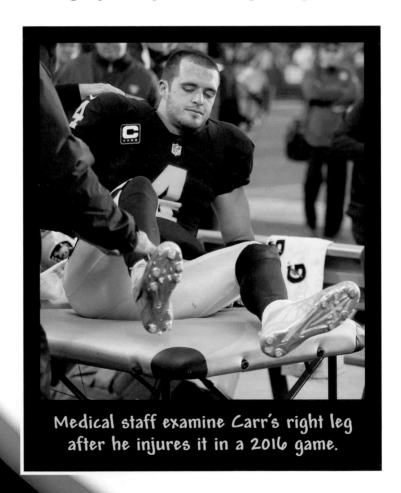

Medical staff examine Carr's right leg after he injures it in a 2016 game.

Carr (left) stretches with teammate Michael Crabtree during a training session in 2017.

two months of **rehab** before his leg was back to normal. He was back in the gym by February. A fan spotted him working out near Oakland and posted a photo on Twitter. Carr had a bandage on his injured leg. But he looked strong and was lifting weights with his legs. Raiders fans sighed with relief. Their star quarterback would be back on the field for the 2017 season.

Carr and his wife, Heather, pose for a photo in 2017.

Carr has a strong faith in God. He says it's the reason he plays football. He tries to live a Christian lifestyle on and off the field. Carr also says his religion helped him deal with his son Dallas's illness and surgeries. He and his wife welcomed a second son, Deker Luke Carr, in March 2016.

Carr (center) attends an event for a new
Valley Children's Healthcare center in 2017.

The doctors and nurses at Valley Children's Hospital in Madera, California, saved Dallas's life. The hospital cares for any children in need in the area. They help children even if their families cannot pay for the care.

In August 2016, Derek and Heather Carr began the DC4KIDS program. The program helps Valley Children's get the best doctors and medical equipment. "We want to make sure Valley Children's is around for other families, just like it was for mine," he said.

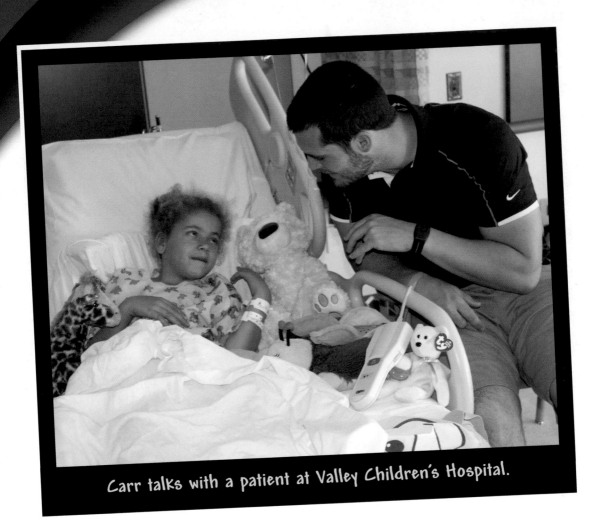
Carr talks with a patient at Valley Children's Hospital.

Carr and his wife take part in a variety of events for the program. They made it possible for a group of kids to go to a Raiders game. The young fans even got to hang out on the field as the team warmed up. Carr often visits the hospital to spend time with sick children. He also appears in commercials and asks people to give money to the hospital.

If you ask Raiders fans who their favorite superhero is, they might say Derek Carr. He would give a different answer: Batman. Carr wore a Batman T-shirt under his football gear throughout high school and college. He even named his dog Bruce Wayne.

Carr's brothers are also superhero fans. Darren Carr likes the Incredible Hulk. David Carr, who favors Superman, paid for a painting that hangs in the living room at their parents' house. The artwork

Raiders fans are known for wearing costumes to games. These Raiders fans are superhero fans too, just like the Carr brothers!

shows the bodies of Batman, the Incredible Hulk, and Superman with the three brothers' faces.

Carr works with a student during a Carr Elite Football Clinic at Bakersfield Christian High School.

Carr wants to help young athletes too. When he was getting ready for the NFL Scouting Combine, he worked out with his oldest brother and their father. With the help of a fitness coach, they put together a program that worked for Carr. The program was such a success that they thought it could help athletes from any sport. So that's what they decided to do. Carr Elite in California is a training center for athletes. It helps athletes get fit and eat more healthful food.

Carr Elite also hosts football camps around California for players from elementary school to college. Carr and his family often take part in the camps. They pass on the lessons they learned in the NFL and in life. "We want to make this game fun and help them become better quarterbacks and better people," Carr said.

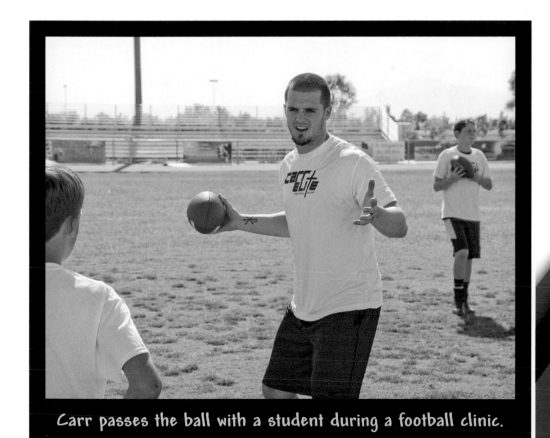

Carr passes the ball with a student during a football clinic.

Carr looks for a receiver during a 2014 game against the Houston Texans.

The Raiders had veteran quarterback Matt Schaub when Carr joined the team in 2014. Most fans expected Schaub to begin the season as the starting quarterback. But Carr played better than Schaub in practice. In September, Raiders coaches announced that Carr would be the starter.

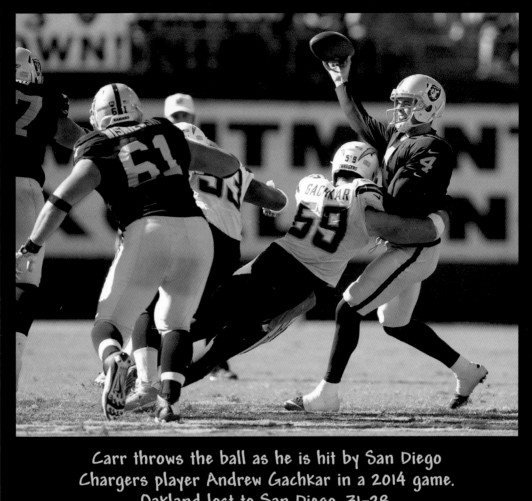

Carr throws the ball as he is hit by San Diego
Chargers player Andrew Gachkar in a 2014 game.
Oakland lost to San Diego, 31–28.

The young quarterback threw 21 touchdowns and 12 interceptions that year. It was a pretty good start to a career. Yet the Raiders were a bad team. Their 3–13 record was second worst in the league in 2014.

Carr threw 32 touchdowns in 2015 and helped the Raiders to a 7–9 record. In 2016, the team was on its way to one of the best records in the NFL. Then Carr broke his leg. Oakland finished the year 12–4 and made the playoffs for the first time in 14 years. But they weren't the same without their superstar quarterback. They lost in the playoffs to the team Carr grew up with, the Houston Texans, 27–14.

It was a tough loss for Oakland. Yet the team's future is bright. Carr made a full recovery from his injury, and he has his sights set on the Super Bowl. "I'm ready to rock," he said. "I'm ready to do absolutely everything."

The Raiders have been to the Super Bowl five times. They've won the big game three times. But they haven't had a Super Bowl victory since 1984, seven years before Carr was born.

Carr celebrates a win in 2016. He says he's excited for even more Oakland wins in 2017.

All-Star Stats

Carr has taken Oakland by storm in just three seasons with the team. In fact, he already ranks highly in many of the team's all-time stats. Take a look at how his touchdown totals compare to other Raiders quarterbacks through the 2016 season:

Most Passing Touchdowns in Oakland Raiders History

Player	Number of passing touchdowns
Ken Stabler	150
Daryle Lamonica	148
Rich Gannon	114
Tom Flores	92
Derek Carr	81
Jim Plunkett	80
Marc Wilson	77
Jeff Hostetler	69
Jay Schroeder	66
Kerry Collins	41
Cotton Davidson	41

Source Notes

6 Associated Press, "Carr Leads Another Rally for Raiders in 38–24 Win over Bills," *ESPN*, December 5, 2016, http://www.espn.com/nfl/recap?gameId=400874724.

10 Ron Kroichick, "Derek Carr's Values, Football Savvy Instilled by His Family," *San Francisco Chronicle*, December 23, 2016, http://www.sfchronicle.com/raiders/article/Derek-Carr-s-values-football-savvy-instilled-10816458.php.

12 Daniel Brown, "Raiders Rookie Derek Carr Has Faced Bigger Tests," *San Jose Mercury News*, last modified August 12, 2016, http://www.mercurynews.com/2014/09/05/raiders-rookie-derek-carr-has-faced-bigger-tests/.

14 "*Sports Illustrated* Rising Stars—David Carr," Vimeo video, 8:08, posted by Val Morgan Outdoor Active, August 24, 2015, https://vimeo.com/album/3441621/video/137109628.

16 Marcus Kwesi O'Mard, "Derek Carr Was Mic'd Up When He Injured Leg, Unforgettably Cries 'It's Broke,'" *NESN*, December 29, 2016, http://nesn.com/2016/12/derek-carr-micd-up-when-he-injured-leg-unforgettably-cries-its-broke.

19 "Oakland Raiders Quarterback Derek Carr Announces Launch of DC4KIDS, Campaign with Valley Children's," *ABC News*, August 25, 2016, http://www.turnto23.com/news/local-news/oakland-raiders-quarterback-derek-carr-announces-launch-of-dc4kids-campaign-with-valley-childrens.

23 Vic Tafur, "Carr Family of Quarterbacks Passes on Its Knowledge to Kids," *SFGATE*, July 8, 2015, http://www.sfgate.com/raiders/article/Carr-family-of-quarterbacks-passes-on-its-6371646.php.

26 Paul Gutierrez, "Derek Carr Full Participant in Raiders' Offseason Training Program," *ESPN*, April 18, 2017, http://www.espn.com/nfl/story/_/id/19181264/oakland-raiders-qb-derek-carr-ready-team-offseason-training-program.

Glossary

center: the player in the middle of the offensive line. The center snaps the ball to the quarterback.

interceptions: passes caught by the opposing team

intestines: the lower part of a person's digestive system

mascots: people dressed up in costumes to represent teams

offensive line: the five players at the front of the offense whose main job is to block defenders

prospect: a person who is likely to succeed

rehab: the process of returning to health

rookie: a first-year player

scouts: people who judge the skills of athletes

vertical jump: jumping straight up from a standing position

veteran: a longtime player

wide receiver: a player whose main job is to catch passes

Further Information

Braun, Eric. *Super Football Infographics*. Minneapolis: Lerner Publications, 2015.

Derek Carr
http://www.derekcarrqb.com

Football: National Football League
http://www.ducksters.com/sports/national_football_league.php

Morey, Allan. *The Oakland Raiders Story*. Minneapolis: Bellwether Media, 2017.

NFL Rush
http://www.nflrush.com

Savage, Jeff. *Football Super Stats*. Minneapolis: Lerner Publications, 2018.

Index

Photo Acknowledgments

The images in this book are used with the permission of: Brian Blanco/Getty Images, p. 2 (background); iStock.com/iconeer, p. 4 (gold star page numbers throughout); Thearon W. Henderson/Getty Images, pp. 4–5, 6; Brian Bahr/Getty Images, pp. 7, 16, 24; Scott Halleran/Getty Images, p. 8; Stephen Dunn/Getty Images, p. 9; AP Photo/ Houston Chronicle, Eddy Matchette, p. 10; Craig Kohlruss/Fresno Bee/MCT/Getty Images, p. 11; AP Photo/Nam Y. Huh, p. 13; Joe Robbins/Getty Images, p. 14; AP Photo/Marcio Jose Sanchez, p. 17; Allen Berezovsky/WireImage for Fashion Media/ Getty Images, p. 18; Joan Barnett Lee/ZUMA Press/Newscom, p. 19; Courtesy Valley Children's Healthcare, p. 20; Ken Murray/Icon Sportswire/Getty Images, p. 21; DC Elite, LLC, pp. 22, 23; Ezra Shaw/Getty Images, p. 25; Jonathan Bachman/Getty Images, p. 27.

Cover: Brian Blanco/Getty Images.